HIS Story

THE FAMILY PICTURE BOOK

ILLUSTRATED BY
MARK LUDY

EDITED & COMPILED BY
KYLE BOSTOCK, MATT MYERS & ROGER STORMS

REAL LIFE
MINISTRIES

HIS
Story©

First Edition - May 2016

Published by Real Life Ministries, Post Falls, ID 83854

Produced in partnership with HIS Story LLC,
based on the work of Matt Myers.

Ludy, Mark. Bostock, Kyle. Myers, Matt. Storms, Roger.
- His Story; The Family Picture Book
Edited and Compiled by Kyle Bostock.
Matt Myers. Roger Storms / Cover art and interior illustra-
tions by Mark Ludy, 1st Ed. p.cm.

Library of Congress Control Number: 2015956975

ISBN: 978-0-692-56497-4

Printed in Canada

Many people have set out to write accounts about the events that have been fulfilled by Jesus Christ. The book you now hold in your hands is one such account. Using the eyewitness accounts of the gospels of Matthew, Mark, Luke and John this picture book seeks to introduce families to the life and ministry of the Savior, Jesus Christ. We pray that as you read this account together, that you may come to know Jesus like never before.

"In the beginning the Word already existed. The Word was with God, and the Word was God. He existed in the beginning with God. God created everything through him, and nothing was created except through him. The Word gave life to everything that was created, and his life brought light to everyone. The light shines in the darkness, and the darkness can never extinguish it. God sent a man, John the Baptist, to tell about the light so that everyone might believe because of his testimony. John himself was not the light; he was simply a witness to tell about the light. The one who is the true light, who gives light to everyone, was coming into the world. He came into the very world he created, but the world didn't recognize him. He came to his own people, and even they rejected him. But to all who believed him and accepted him, he gave the right to become children of God. They are reborn -- not with a physical birth resulting from human passion or plan, but a birth that comes from God. So the Word became human and made his home among us. He was full of unfailing love and faithfulness. And we have seen his glory, the glory of the Father's one and only Son. John testified about him when he shouted to the crowds, "This is the one I was talking about when I said, 'Someone is coming after me who is

far greater than I am, for he existed long before me.'" From his abundance we have all received one gracious blessing after another. For the law was given through Moses, but God's unfailing love and faithfulness came through Jesus Christ. No one has ever seen God. But the unique One, who is himself God, is near to the Father's heart. He has revealed God to us."

-- Written by John, one of Jesus' disciples
  John 1:1-18 NLT

Chapter 1
THE BIRTH OF HOPE

In those days, God sent the angel Gabriel to a young woman named Mary, who was engaged to be married to a man named Joseph, a descendant of King David.

Gabriel appeared to Mary and said, "Greetings, favored woman! The Lord is with you!"

Confused and disturbed, Mary tried to think what the angel could mean.

"Don't be afraid, Mary," the angel told her, "for you have found favor with God! You will become pregnant and give birth to a son, and you will name him Jesus. The Lord God will give him the throne of his ancestor David. And his Kingdom will never end!"

Mary asked the angel, "But how can this happen? I am a virgin."

The angel replied, "Nothing is impossible with God."

Mary responded, "I am the Lord's servant. May everything you have said about me come true."

And then the angel left her.

Before Mary and Joseph were married, Mary become pregnant just as the angel Gabriel had promised. Joseph was upset and confused by the news of Mary's pregnancy.

That night an angel of the Lord appeared to him in a dream saying, "do not be afraid to take Mary as your wife. For the child within her is from the Holy Spirit. And she will have a son, and you are to name him Jesus, for he will save his people from their sins."

When Joseph woke up, he did as the angel had commanded him and took Mary as his wife.

Some time later the Roman emperor, Augustus, decreed that a census should be taken throughout the Roman Empire. Because Joseph was a descendant of King David, he had to go to Bethlehem in Judea, King David's hometown, to complete the census. Traveling from his home in Nazareth, Joseph took Mary with him to Bethlehem.

While they were there, the time came for her baby to be born. She gave birth to a son, and named him Jesus. She wrapped him snugly in strips of cloth and laid him in a manger, because there was no lodging available for them.

Luke 1:2; 3:23-38; John 1:2; Matthew 1:1

Meanwhile, that very night there were shepherds staying in the fields nearby, guarding their flocks of sheep. Suddenly, an angel of the Lord appeared among them, and the radiance of the Lord's glory surrounded them.

They were terrified.

"Don't be afraid!" the angel said. "I bring you good news that will bring great joy to all people. The Savior has been born today in Bethlehem! You will find a baby wrapped in strips of cloth, lying in a manger."

Suddenly, the angel was joined by the armies of heaven praising God and saying, "Glory to God in highest, and peace on earth."

When the angels had returned to heaven, the shepherds said to each other, "Let's go to Bethlehem and see the Savior, which the Lord has told us about."

They hurried to the village and found Mary and Joseph with the baby, lying in the manger. The shepherds told everyone what had happened and what the angel had said to them about this child.

All who heard the shepherds' story were astonished, but Mary kept all these things in her heart and thought about them often. The shepherds went back to their flocks, glorifying and praising God because everything they had heard and seen was just as the angel had told them.

Some time later wise men from eastern lands arrived in Jerusalem, asking, "Where is the newborn king of the Jews? We saw his star as it rose, and we have come to worship him."

The star they had seen in the east guided them to Bethlehem, and stopped over the place where the child was. Filled with joy, they entered the house and saw the child with his mother, Mary, and they bowed down and worshiped him. Then they opened their treasure chests and gave him gifts of gold, frankincense, and myrrh.

In the years to come Jesus grew in wisdom and in stature and in favor with God and everyone who knew him.

Chapter 2

JESUS' MINISTRY BEGINS

Years later a man the people called John the Baptist came to the Judean wilderness, preaching that everyone should turn from their sins and be baptized.

He cried out to the people, "Repent of your sins and turn to God, for the Kingdom of Heaven is near."

John's clothes were woven from coarse camel hair, and he ate locusts and wild honey for food.

The prophet Isaiah had written about John hundreds of years before saying, "Look, I am sending my messenger ahead of you, and he will prepare your way. He is a voice shouting in the wilderness, 'Prepare the way for the LORD's coming! Clear the road for him!' "

People from all over Israel went out to see John and listen to his teaching. As they listened they were moved by the Holy Spirit. They confessed their sins, and John baptized them in the Jordan River.

One day as John was preaching, Jesus came to be baptized by John.

John, realizing that Jesus was the coming Savior, exclaimed, "I am the one who needs to be baptized by you. So why are you coming to me?"

(John had said that one day someone greater than he would come whose sandals he would not be worthy to untie.)

But Jesus replied, "It should be done, for we must carry out all that God requires."

So John baptized Jesus in the Jordan River.

As Jesus came up out of the water, the heavens opened, and the Holy Spirit descended on him like a dove. And a voice from heaven said, "You are my dearly loved Son, and you bring me great joy."

Then Jesus, full of the Holy Spirit, was led into the wilderness to be tempted there by the devil. Jesus was in the wilderness for forty days and forty nights. He ate nothing and became very hungry. During this time the devil came to tempt Jesus offering him food and fame and fortune if Jesus would just bow down and worship him.

Chapter 3

THE DISCIPLES FOLLOW JESUS

One day as Jesus was preaching on the shore of the Sea of Galilee, a huge crowd gathered around him to listen to him proclaim the word of God. As he was teaching he noticed two brothers - Simon Peter and Andrew - who had left their boats and were washing their nets on the shore.

As the crowds pushed in, Jesus stepped into one of the boats and asked Simon to push it out into the water. Jesus taught the crowds while sitting in the boat.

When he was finished speaking, Jesus said to Simon, "Now go out where it is deeper, and let down your nets to catch some fish."

"Master," Simon Peter replied, "we worked hard all last night and didn't catch a thing. But if you say so, I'll let the nets down again."

When Simon Peter went to pull in his nets they were so full of fish that they began to tear! The fish filled his boat to the point of almost sinking.

Awestruck, Simon Peter fell to his knees before Jesus and exclaimed, "Oh, Lord, please leave me -- I'm too much

of a sinner to be around you,"

Jesus replied, "Don't be afraid! Come, follow me, and I will show you how to fish for people!"

And as soon as they landed, Simon Peter and Andrew left everything and followed Jesus.

A little farther up the shore Jesus saw two other brothers, James and John, sitting in a boat with their father, repairing their nets. Jesus called to them saying, "Come follow me." Immediately they followed him, leaving their father in the boat.

Jesus and his new followers went from town to town teaching in the synagogues and healing the sick. As people listened to Jesus, they were amazed by his teaching. The news about Jesus spread quickly throughout the land. Huge crowds gathered around Jesus wherever he went to hear him preach and to be healed of their diseases.

One day the house where he was staying was so packed with visitors that there was no more room, even outside the door.

Four men came carrying a paralyzed man on a sleeping mat. They tried to take him inside to Jesus, but they couldn't reach him because of the crowd. So they went up to the roof and dug a hole through the roof above his head. Then they lowered the sick man on his mat down into the crowd, right in front of Jesus.

Seeing their faith, Jesus said to the man, "Young man, your sins are forgiven."

But the Pharisees and teachers of religious law said to themselves, "Who does he think he is? That's blasphemy! Only God can forgive sins!"

Jesus knew immediately what they were thinking, so he asked them, "Why do you question this in your hearts? Is it easier to say to the paralyzed man 'Your sins are forgiven,' or 'Stand up, pick up your mat, and walk'? So I will prove to you that the Son of Man has the authority on earth to forgive sins."

Then Jesus turned to the paralyzed man and said, "Stand up, pick up your mat, and go home!"

And immediately, as everyone watched, the man jumped up, picked up his mat, and went home praising God. Everyone was gripped with great wonder and awe, and they praised God for sending a man with such great authority, proclaiming, "We have seen amazing things today!"

Then Jesus went out to the lakeshore again and taught the crowds that were coming to him. As he walked along, he saw Levi sitting at his tax collector's booth.

"Follow me and be my disciple," Jesus said to him.

So Levi got up, left everything, and followed him.

Jesus chose twelve men to be his apostles. They were to accompany him, and he would send them out to preach, giving them authority to do miracles.

Here are their names: Simon Peter, James and John (the sons of Zebedee), Andrew, Philip, Bartholomew, Matthew, also known as Levi, Thomas, James (son of Alphaeus), Thaddaeus, Simon (the zealot), and Judas Iscariot (who later betrayed him).

Simon Peter

Chapter 4
THE SERMON ON THE MOUNT

People came from all over to hear Jesus' teaching about the Kingdom of God. One day as Jesus saw the crowds gathering, he went up on the mountainside and sat down. His disciples gathered around him, and he began to teach them.

"God blesses those who are poor and realize their need for him, for the Kingdom of Heaven is theirs. God blesses those who mourn, for they will be comforted. God blesses those who are humble, for they will inherit the whole earth. God blesses those who hunger and thirst for justice, for they will be satisfied. God blesses those who are merciful, for they will be shown mercy. God blesses those whose hearts are pure, for they will see God. God blesses those who work for peace, for they will be called the children of God. God blesses those who are persecuted for doing right, for the Kingdom of Heaven is theirs."

Jesus taught them that they could show others what God's kingdom looked like by they way they lived their lives.

He continued his teaching saying, "You are the salt of the earth. But what good is salt if it has lost its flavor? Can you make it salty again? It will be thrown out and trampled underfoot as worthless. You are the light of the world—like a city on a hilltop that cannot be hidden. No one lights a lamp and then puts it under a basket. Instead, a lamp is placed on a stand, where it gives light to everyone in the house. In the same way, let your good deeds shine out for all to see, so that everyone will praise your heavenly Father"

Jesus taught his disciples that when they pray they should pray like this, "Our Father in heaven, may your name be kept holy. May your Kingdom come soon. May your will be done on earth, as it is in heaven. Give us today the food we need, and forgive us our sins, as we have forgiven those who sin against us. And don't let us yield to temptation, but rescue us from the evil one."

Jesus challenged his disciples to live differently than those around them. "Don't store up treasures here on earth, where moths eat them and rust destroys them, and where thieves break in and steal. Store your treasures in heaven, where moths and rust cannot destroy, and thieves do not break in and steal. Wherever your treasure is, there the desires of your heart will also be."

John 5, Matthew 12:1-21, 5:1-7:1-28; Mark 1:23-3:19, Luke 6:1-26, Acts

"Seek the Kingdom of God above all else, and live righteously, and he will give you everything you need. So don't worry about tomorrow, for tomorrow will bring its own worries. Today's trouble is enough for today. Forgive others, and you will be forgiven. Give, and you will receive. For you will be treated as you treat others."

"Do to others whatever you would like them to do to you. This is the essence of all that is taught in the law and the prophets."

Jesus finished his teaching saying, "Anyone who listens to my teaching and follows it is wise, like a person who builds a house on solid rock. Though the rain comes in torrents and the floodwaters rise and the winds beat against that house, it won't collapse because it is built on bedrock. But anyone who hears my teaching and ignores it is foolish, like a person who builds a house on sand. When the rains and floods come and the winds beat against that house, it will collapse with a mighty crash."

When Jesus had finished saying these things, all the people were amazed by his teaching, because he taught with great authority.

Bartholomew

Philip

Thaddaeus

Chapter 5

JESUS DISPLAYS HIS POWER

When Jesus had finished teaching his disciples, one of the Pharisees invited Jesus into his home for dinner. As dinner was about to begin a woman, who was known to be living a life of sin, came to see Jesus. She brought with her an alabaster jar filled with expensive perfume. The woman knelt behind him at his feet, and began to weep. Her tears ran down her face and fell on Jesus' feet, washing them, and she wiped them off with her hair. As she kissed Jesus' feet, she broke the alabaster jar and covered his feet with the perfume.

When the Pharisee who had invited Jesus saw this, he said to himself, "If this man were a prophet, he would know what kind of woman is touching him. She's a sinner!"

Then Jesus answered his thoughts. "Simon," he said to the Pharisee, "I have something to say to you."

"Go ahead, Teacher," Simon replied.

Then Jesus told him this story: "A man loaned money to two people—500 pieces of silver to one and 50 pieces to the other. But neither of them could repay him, so he kindly forgave them both, canceling their debts. Who do you suppose loved him more after that?"

Simon answered, "I suppose the one for whom he canceled the larger debt."

"That's right," Jesus said.

Then he turned to the woman and said to Simon, "Look at this woman kneeling here. When I entered your home, you didn't offer me water to wash the dust from my feet, but she has washed them with her tears and wiped them with her hair. You didn't greet me with a kiss, but from the time I first came in, she has not stopped kissing my feet. You neglected the courtesy of olive oil to anoint my head, but she has anointed my feet with rare perfume. I tell you, her sins—and they are many—have been forgiven, so she has shown me much love. But a person who is forgiven little shows only little love."

Then Jesus said to the woman, "Your sins are forgiven."

The men at the table said among themselves, "Who is this man, that he goes around forgiving sins?"

And Jesus said to the woman, "Your faith has saved you; go in peace."

As the woman left the house Jesus continued saying, "Come to me, all of you who are weary and carry heavy burdens, and I will give you rest. Take my yoke upon you. Let me teach you, because I am humble and gentle at heart, and you will find rest for your souls. For my yoke is easy to bear, and the burden I give you is light."

That evening, as the crowds gathered around, Jesus said to his disciples, "Let's cross to the other side of the lake." So the disciples took Jesus in the boat leaving the crowds behind.

Along the way a fierce storm came up. Huge waves began to crash against the boat, filing it with water. The disciples became terrified.

All the while, Jesus was sleeping soundly in the back of the boat.

The disciples woke him up, shouting, "Teacher, don't you care that we're going to drown?"

When Jesus woke up, he rebuked the wind and said to the water, "Silence! Be still!"

Suddenly the wind stopped, and there was a great calm. Then he asked them, "Why are you afraid? Do you still have no faith?"

The disciples were terrified by what they had witnessed. "Who is this man?" they asked each other. "Even the wind and waves obey him!"

When Jesus and the disciples arrived at the other side of the lake they were met by a man who had been tormented by evil spirits for years. Having mercy on the man, Jesus cast out the evil spirit and sent them into a herd of 2,000 pigs. The evil spirits caused the pigs to run off a nearby cliff and drown in the water below. The people of that town were concerned by what they had seen. Afraid of Jesus' power, the people asked Jesus to leave that place.

So Jesus and the disciples traveled back across the lake. When they arrived at the shore a man named Jairus fell at Jesus' feet, pleading with Jesus to come to his home.

"My little daughter is dying," he said. "Please come and lay your hands on her; heal her so she can live."

While on their way, messengers met Jairus telling him, "Your daughter is dead. There's no use troubling the Teacher now."

But Jesus overheard them and said to Jairus, "Don't be afraid. Just have faith, and she will be healed."

When they came to Jairus' home, Jesus saw many people weeping for the young girl who had died.

He went inside and asked, "Why all this commotion and weeping? The child isn't dead; she's only asleep."

The crowd laughed at him because they all knew she had died. But he made them all leave, and he took the girl's father and mother and his three disciples into the room where the girl was lying.

Holding her hand, he said to her, "Little girl, get up!"

And the young girl immediately stood up and walked around! All who were there were overwhelmed and totally amazed by Jesus' power.

With this the stories of Jesus' many miracles and the fame of Jesus' power swept through the entire countryside.

Matthew
Also known as Levi

Chapter 6

THE DISCIPLES LEARN TO TRUST JESUS

Jesus and his disciples continued their ministry, stopping in all the towns and villages along their way, teaching about the Good News of God's Kingdom, and healing every kind of disease and illness.

As they were going Jesus called his twelve disciples together and said to them, "Unless you take up your cross daily and follow me, you are not worthy of being mine. If you cling to your life, you will lose it; but if you give up your life for me, you will find it."

Then he sent them out two by two, giving them the power and authority to cast out evil spirits and to heal every kind of disease and illness. Commanding them to tell everyone that the Kingdom of Heaven is near.

After some time, the apostles returned to Jesus from their ministry tour. Hearing all that they had done in His name, Jesus said, "Let's go off by ourselves to a quiet place and rest awhile."

So they left that place by boat looking for a quiet place to rest. But when the crowds saw Jesus leaving they ran ahead of him along the shore. As Jesus reached the shore he saw the massive crowd and had compassion on them because they were like sheep without a shepherd.

As the crowds pressed in the disciples came to Jesus and said, "This is a remote place, and it's already getting late. Send the crowds away so they can go to the nearby farms and villages, so they can find food and lodging for the night."

But Jesus said, "You feed them."

"With what?" they asked. "We'd have to work for months to earn enough money to buy food for all these people!"

"How much bread do you have?" he asked. "Go and find out."

They came back and said, "There's a young boy here with five barley loaves and two fish. But what good is that with this huge crowd?

"Bring them here," Jesus said, "and tell everyone to sit down."

As the disciples had the people sit on the grassy slopes, Jesus took the five loaves of bread, looked up to heaven, and gave thanks to God. Breaking the bread into pieces he

began passing it out to the people. Likewise, he did the same with the two fish, until everyone there ate as much as they wanted.

Then Jesus told his disciples, "Now gather the leftovers, so that nothing is wasted."

Gathering up the scraps from all who had eaten, they filled twelve baskets with the leftover food.

Jesus fed 5,000 men that day, not including all the women and children!

Realizing the miracle that they had just witnessed, the people exclaimed, "Surely, he is the Prophet we have been expecting!"

Immediately after this, Jesus insisted that his disciples get back into the boat and cross to the other side of the lake. As they went on their way, Jesus sent the crowds home and slipped away into the hills by himself to pray.

Late that night, while alone praying in the hills, he looked up and noticed that the disciples were in serious trouble. In the middle of the lake, a storm had overtaken them and the disciples were rowing hard and struggling against the wind and waves.

Jesus came toward them, walking on the water.

When the disciples saw him walking on the water, they were terrified.

They cried out, "It's a ghost!"

But Jesus spoke to them.

"Don't be afraid," he said. "Take courage. I am here!"

Then Peter called out, "Lord, if it's really you, tell me to come to you, walking on the water."

"Yes, come," Jesus said.

So Peter went over the side of the boat and walked on the water toward Jesus. But when he saw the strong wind and the waves, he was terrified and began to sink.

"Save me, Lord!" he shouted.

Jesus immediately reached out and grabbed him.

"You have so little faith," Jesus said. "Why did you doubt me?"

When they climbed back into the boat, the wind stopped. Then the disciples worshiped him.

"You really are the Son of God!" they exclaimed.

Then immediately they arrived at their destination!

After their arrival many came from miles around hoping to see Jesus do another miraculous sign as the news of Jesus feeding the 5000 spread.

They came hoping for a meal, but Jesus told them, "I tell you the truth, Moses didn't give you bread from heaven. My Father did. And now he offers you the true bread from heaven. I am the true bread that came down from heaven. Anyone who eats this bread will not die as your ancestors did (even though they ate the manna) but will live forever. I tell you the truth, anyone who believes has eternal life."

At this point many of his disciples turned away and deserted him.

Then Jesus turned to the Twelve and asked, "Are you also going to leave?"

Simon Peter replied, "Lord, to whom would we go? You have the words that give eternal life. We believe, and we know you are the Holy One of God."

Through all of this Jesus' chosen Twelve learned to trust him even when they didn't completely understand.

Chapter 7

THE KINGDOM BELONGS TO THESE

As the news of Jesus' miraculous works continued to spread throughout the land, many people brought their friends who were lame, blind, crippled, mute, and many others. Jesus healed all of them.

Everyone was amazed!

Those who hadn't been able to speak were talking, the crippled were made well, the lame were walking, and the blind could see again!

One day, as Jesus and his disciples were traveling between towns, he asked them, "Who do people say that the Son of Man is?"

"Well," they replied, "some say John the Baptist, some say Elijah, and others say Jeremiah or one of the other prophets risen from the dead."

Then he asked them, "But who do you say I am?"

Simon Peter answered, "You are the Messiah, the Son of the living God."

Jesus replied, "You are blessed, Simon son of John, because my Father in heaven has revealed this to you. You did not learn this from any human being. Now I say to you that you are Peter (which means 'rock'), and upon this rock I will build my church, and all the powers of hell will not conquer it. And I will give you the keys of the Kingdom of Heaven."

Confused by Jesus' statement, the disciples came to Jesus and asked, "Who is the greatest in the Kingdom of Heaven?"

Jesus responded, "Whoever wants to be first must take last place and be the servant of everyone else."

As Jesus continued teaching, some parents brought their children to him so that he could lay his hands on them and pray for them. Irritated by the interruption, the disciples scolded the parents for bothering Jesus while he was teaching.

But Jesus said, "Let the children come to me. Don't stop them! For the Kingdom of Heaven belongs to those who are like these children."

Then Jesus, turning to the little children who were among them, said, "I tell you the truth, unless you turn

from your sins and become like little children, you will never get into the Kingdom of Heaven. So anyone who becomes as humble as this little child is the greatest in the Kingdom of Heaven. Anyone who welcomes a little child like this on my behalf welcomes me, and anyone who welcomes me also welcomes my Father who sent me. Whoever is the least among you is the greatest."

At this, Jesus placed his hands on the children's heads and blessed them.

"Beware that you don't look down on any of these little ones," Jesus continued. "If a man has a hundred sheep and one of them wanders away, what will he do? Won't he leave the ninety-nine others on the hills and go out to search for the one that is lost? And if he finds it, I tell you the truth, he will rejoice over it more than over the ninety-nine that didn't wander away! In the same way, it is not my heavenly Father's will that even one of these little ones should perish."

After this, Jesus took Peter, James, and John up on a high mountain to be alone and pray.

As Jesus was praying, the appearance of his face was transformed so that his face shone like the sun, and his clothes became dazzling white.

Suddenly, Moses and Elijah appeared in a glorious display. They began talking with Jesus about all that would happen in Jerusalem over the coming weeks as Jesus completed his mission on earth.

Meanwhile, Peter and the others had fallen asleep. When they woke up, they saw Jesus' glory and the two men standing with him.

Then a voice from heaven said, "This is my dearly loved Son, who brings me great joy. Listen to him."

The disciples were terrified and fell face down on the ground.

Jesus came over and put his arms around his disciples.

"Get up," he said. "Don't be afraid."

When they finally had the courage to look up they saw only Jesus.

James
Son of Zebedee

Chapter 8

THE GOOD SAMARITAN

One morning, as Jesus was teaching in the Temple, a large crowd gathered around to listen to his teaching.

While he was teaching, the teachers of religious law and the Pharisees brought a woman who had been caught sinning and put her in front of the crowd.

"Teacher," they said to Jesus, "this woman was caught in the act of adultery. The law of Moses says to stone her. What do you say?"

They were trying to trap him into saying something they could use against him, but Jesus stooped down and wrote in the dust with his finger.

They kept demanding an answer, so he stood up again and said, "All right, but let the one who has never sinned throw the first stone!"

Then he stooped down again and wrote in the dust.

When the accusers heard this, they slipped away one by one, beginning with the oldest, until only Jesus was left with the woman near the crowd.

Then Jesus stood up again and said to the woman, "Where are your accusers? Didn't even one of them condemn you?"

"No, Lord," she said.

And Jesus said, "Neither do I. Go and sin no more."

Then Jesus said to the crowd, "I am the light of the world. If you follow me, you won't have to walk in darkness, because you will have the light that leads to life. You are truly my disciples if you remain faithful to my teachings. And you will know the truth, and the truth will set you free."

Some time later another teacher of the Law came to test Jesus by asking him this question, "Teacher, what should I do to inherit eternal life?"

Jesus replied, "What does the law of Moses say? How do you read it?"

The man answered, "'You must love the Lord your God with all your heart, all your soul, all your strength, and all your mind.' And, 'Love your neighbor as yourself.'"

"Right!" Jesus told him. "Do this and

John 7:11-10:42, *Matthew* 8:19-22, 12:22-45, *Luke* 9:57-14:24, *Mark* 3:20-30

you will live!"

Wanting to justify his actions he asked Jesus, "And who is my neighbor?"

Jesus replied with this story, "A Jewish man was traveling on a trip from Jerusalem to Jericho, and he was attacked by bandits. They stripped him of his clothes, beat him up, and left him half dead beside the road. By chance a priest came along. But when he saw the man lying there, he crossed to the other side of the road and passed him by. A Temple assistant walked over and looked at him lying there, but he also passed by on the other side. Then a despised Samaritan came along, and when he saw the man, he felt compassion for him. Going over to him, the Samaritan soothed his wounds with olive oil and wine and bandaged them. Then he put the man on his own donkey and took him to an inn, where he took care of him. The next day he handed the innkeeper two silver coins, telling him, 'Take care of this man. If his bill runs higher than this, I'll pay you the next time I'm here.'"

"Now which of these three would you say was a neighbor to the man who was attacked by bandits?" Jesus asked.

The man replied, "The one who showed him mercy."

Then Jesus said, "Yes, now go and do the same."

Chapter 9

JESUS' POWER OVER SIN AND DEATH

As Jesus continued his ministry, many notorious sinners came to listen to his teaching. This bothered the Pharisees and teachers of religious law. They did not understand why Jesus would associate with such sinful people.

So Jesus, knowing their heart, told them this story...

"A man had two sons. The younger son told his father, 'I want my share of your estate now before you die.' So his father agreed to divide his wealth between his sons."

"A few days later, this younger son packed all his belongings and moved to a distant land, and there he wasted all his money in wild living. About the time his money ran out, a great famine swept over the land, and he began to starve. He persuaded a local farmer to hire him, and the man sent him into his fields to feed the pigs. The young man became so hungry that even the pods he was feeding the pigs looked good to him. But no one gave him anything."

"When he finally came to his senses, he said to himself, 'At home even the hired servants have food enough to spare, and here I am dying of hunger! I will go home to my father and say, 'Father, I have sinned against both heaven and you, and I am no longer worthy of being called your son. Please take me on as a hired servant.'"

"So he returned home to his father. And while he was still a long way off, his father saw him coming. Filled with love and compassion, he ran to his son, embraced him, and kissed him. His son said to him, 'Father, I have sinned against both heaven and you, and I am no longer worthy of being called your son.'"

"But his father said to the servants, 'Quick! Bring the finest robe in the house and put it on him. Get a ring for his finger and sandals for his feet. And kill the calf we have been fattening. We must celebrate with a feast, for this son of mine was dead and has now returned to life. He was lost, but now he is found.' So the party began.

"Meanwhile, the older son was in the fields working. When he returned home, he heard music and dancing in the house, and he asked one of the servants what was going on. 'Your brother is back,' he was told, 'and your father has killed the fattened calf. We

gave me even one young goat for a feast with my friends. Yet when this son of yours comes back after squandering your money...you celebrate by killing the fattened calf!'"

"His father said to him, 'Look, dear son, you have always stayed by me, and everything I have is yours. We had to celebrate this happy day. For your brother was dead and has come back to life! He was lost, but now he is found!'"

As Jesus was finishing his story a messenger came with word that Jesus' dear friend Lazarus, the brother of Mary and Martha, was very sick.

Hearing the news of Lazarus' sickness Jesus said to his disciples, "Let's go back to Judea, our friend Lazarus has fallen asleep, but now I will go and wake him up."

When Jesus finally arrived at the home of Mary and Martha, he was told that Lazarus had already been in his grave for four days.

Martha said to Jesus, "Lord, if only you had been here, my brother would not have died. But even now I know that God will give you whatever you ask."

Jesus told her, "Your brother will rise again."

"Yes," Martha said, "he will rise when everyone else rises, at the last day."

are celebrating because of his safe return.'

"The older brother was angry and wouldn't go in. His father came out and begged him, but he replied, 'All these years I've slaved for you and never once refused to do a single thing you told me to. And in all that time you never

Then Jesus told her, "I am the resurrection and the life. Anyone who believes in me will live, even after dying. Everyone who lives in me and believes in me will never ever die. Do you believe this, Martha?"

"Yes, Lord," she told him. "I have always believed you are the Messiah, the Son of God, the one who has come into the world from God."

Likewise, when Mary saw Jesus, she fell at his feet and said, "Lord, if only you had been here, my brother would not have died."

When Jesus saw her weeping and saw the other people wailing with her, a deep anger welled up within him, and he was deeply troubled.

"Where have you put him?" he asked them.

They told him, "Lord, come and see."

Then Jesus wept.

Jesus was still angry as he arrived at the tomb, a cave with a stone rolled across its entrance.

"Roll the stone aside," Jesus told them.

But Martha protested, "Lord, he has been dead for four days. The smell will be terrible."

Jesus responded, "Didn't I tell you that you would see God's glory if you believe?"

So they rolled the stone aside.

Then Jesus looked up to heaven and said, "Father, thank you for hearing me. You always hear me, but I said it out loud for the sake of all these people standing here, so that they will believe you sent me."

Then Jesus shouted, "Lazarus, come out!"

At this Lazarus came out in grave clothes, with his face wrapped in a headcloth.

Jesus told them, "Unwrap him and let him go!"

When they saw that Jesus had raised Lazarus from the dead, many people believed that Jesus was the promised Savior.

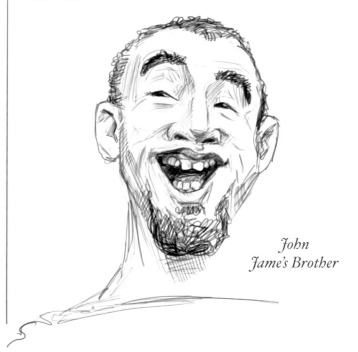

John
Jame's Brother

Chapter 10
THE TRIUMPHAL ENTRY

Knowing that his ministry on earth was coming to an end, Jesus set his eyes towards Jerusalem.

As Jesus and his disciples approached the city he sent two of them on ahead.

"Go into that village over there," he told them. "As soon as you enter it, you will see a young donkey tied there that no one has ever ridden. Untie it and bring it here. If anyone asks, 'What are you doing?' just say, 'The Lord needs it and will return it soon.' "

The two disciples left at once and, upon entering the village, they found the colt standing in the street just as Jesus had told them.

As they were untying the colt, some people standing nearby questioned, "What are you doing, untying that colt?"

They replied, "The Lord needs it."

So they were allowed to take the colt back to Jesus. The disciples placed their garments on the colt, and Jesus rode the colt into Jerusalem.

This happened to fulfill the prophecy,

"Tell the people of Israel, 'Look, your King is coming to you. He is humble, riding on a donkey -- riding on a donkey's colt.' "

As Jesus entered the city, the people spread their garments and palm branches on the road ahead of him. Many in the crowd had seen Jesus raise Lazarus from the dead and had invited others to come and meet him.

The crowd began to shout and sing as they walked along, "Praise God for the Son of David! Blessings on the one who comes in the name of the LORD! Praise God in highest heaven!"

But some of the Pharisees among the crowd complained, "Teacher, rebuke your followers for saying things like that!"

Jesus replied, "If they kept quiet, the stones along the road would burst into cheers!"

The entire city of Jerusalem was in an uproar as he entered. The blind and the lame came to him in the Temple, and he healed them. The leading priests and the teachers of religious law saw these wonderful miracles and heard

even the children in the Temple shouting, "Praise God for the Son of David."

This made the religious leaders furious.

They asked Jesus, "Do you hear what these children are saying?"

"Yes," Jesus replied. "Haven't you ever read the Scriptures? For they say, 'You have taught children and infants to give you praise.' "

Then a voice spoke from heaven, saying, "I have already brought glory to my name, and I will do so again."

When the crowd heard the voice, some thought it was thunder, while others declared an angel had spoken.

Then Jesus told them, "The voice was for your benefit, not mine. The time for judging this world has come, when Satan, the ruler of this world, will be cast out. And when I am lifted up from the earth, I will draw everyone to myself."

When Jesus had finished saying all these things, he said to his disciples, "As you know, Passover begins in two days, and the Son of Man will be handed over to be crucified."

At the very same time the leading priests and elders were meeting, discussing how to capture Jesus secretly and kill him.

As they were plotting, Judas Iscariot

one of the twelve disciples, came to them and asked, "How much will you pay me to betray Jesus to you?"

They agreed to give Judas thirty pieces of silver.

Judas agreed to the deal and began looking for an opportunity to betray Jesus so they could arrest him.

*James
Son of Alphaus*

*Simon
The Zealot*

Chapter 11

THE LAST SUPPER

On the first day of the Festival of Unleavened Bread, Jesus sent Peter and John, into Jerusalem to prepare for the Passover meal, with these instructions:

"As you go into the city, a man carrying a pitcher of water will meet you. Follow him. At the house he enters, say to the owner, 'The Teacher says: My time has come. Where is the guest room where I can eat the Passover meal with my disciples?' He will take you upstairs to a large room that is already set up. That is where you should prepare our meal."

As they entered the city they found everything just as Jesus had said, and they prepared the Passover meal in the upper room just as Jesus had commanded.

That evening as Jesus and the disciples sat down for the Passover meal together, Jesus said, "I have been very eager to eat this Passover meal with you before my suffering begins. For I tell you now that I won't eat this meal again until its meaning is fulfilled in the Kingdom of God."

With that Jesus got up from the table, took off his robe, wrapped a towel around his waist, and poured water into a basin. Then he began to wash the disciples' feet.

When Jesus came to Peter he said, "Lord, are you going to wash my feet?"

Jesus replied, "You don't understand now what I am doing, but someday you will."

"No," Peter protested, "you will never ever wash my feet!"

Jesus replied, "Unless I wash you, you won't belong to me."

Peter exclaimed, "Then wash my hands and head as well, Lord, not just my feet!"

After Jesus had finished washing the disciples feet, he said, "You call me ' Teacher' and 'Lord,' and you are right, because that is what I am. And since I, your Lord and Teacher, have washed your feet, you ought to wash each other's feet. I have given you an example to follow. Do as I have done to you. Now that you know these things, God will bless you for doing them."

As they were at the table eating, Jesus was deeply troubled, and he exclaimed, "I tell you the truth, one of you eating

with me here will betray me!"

Concerned, the disciple sitting next to Jesus asked, "Lord, who is it?"

Jesus responded, "It is the one to whom I give the bread I dip in the bowl."

And when he had dipped it, he gave it to Judas.

Then Jesus told Judas, "Hurry and do what you're going to do."

So Judas left the house at once, going out into the night.

Then Jesus took some bread and blessed it. He broke it in pieces and gave it to the disciples, saying, "Take this and eat it, for this is my body. Do this to remember me."

Likewise, after supper, he took a cup of wine and gave thanks to God for it. He gave it to them and said, "Each of you drink from it, to remember me. For this is my blood, which confirms the new covenant between God and his people. It is poured out as a sacrifice to forgive the sins of many. Mark my words -- I will not drink wine again until the day I drink it new with you in my Father's Kingdom."

After all the disciples had drank from the cup, Jesus began to teach them saying, "So now I am giving you a new commandment: Love each other. Just as I have loved you, you should love each other. Your love for one another will prove to the world that you are my disciples."

"I am the true grapevine, and my Father is the gardener. Yes, I am the vine; you are the branches. Those who remain in me, and I in them, will produce much fruit. For apart from me you can do nothing. But if you remain in me and my words remain in you, you may ask for anything you want, and it will be granted! When you produce much fruit, you are my true disciples. This brings great glory to my Father. I have loved you even as the Father has loved me. Remain in my love."

After finishing his teaching, Jesus left that Upper Room and took the disciples to the garden of Gethsemane to spend that night praying as he did often.

Andrew
Peter's Brother

Chapter 12

THE CRUCIFIXION

Arriving at the Garden of Gethsemane, Jesus commanded his disciples, "Sit here while I go over there to pray. Pray that you will not give in to temptation."

Taking Peter, James and John, with him to a secluded place he told them, "My soul is crushed with grief to the point of death. Stay here and keep watch with me."

Going a little further Jesus fell with his face to the ground and cried out, "Abba, Father, everything is possible for you. Please take this cup of suffering away from me. Yet I want your will to be done, not mine."

As the agony of what was about to come overtook him, Jesus prayed even more fervently and his sweat fell to the ground like great drops of blood.

After he had finished praying, Jesus returned to the disciples and found them asleep, exhausted from grief.

Jesus said to them, "The time has come. The Son of Man is betrayed into the hands of sinners. Up, let's be going."

Meanwhile, Judas, knowing where Jesus and the disciples would be, brought guards to arrest him.

Walking up to Jesus, Judas exclaimed,

"Greetings, Rabbi!" Then Judas gave Jesus a kiss of greeting.

Judas Iscariot

Jesus replied, "Judas, would you betray the Son of Man with a kiss? My friend, go ahead and do what you have come for."

Then the guards grabbed Jesus and arrested him.

Simon Peter, hoping to rescue Jesus, pulled out his sword and struck the servant of the High Priest, cutting off his ear.

"No more of this. Put away your sword," Jesus shouted. "Those who use the sword will die by the sword. Shall I not drink from the cup of suffering the Father has given me? Don't you realize that I could ask my Father for thousands of angels to protect us, and he would send them instantly? But if I did, how would the Scriptures be fulfilled that describe what must happen now?"

Then Jesus touched the servant's ear and healed him.

At this, Jesus' disciples fled from the garden.

The guards then took Jesus to be put on trial before Caiaphas, the high priest. Caiaphas said to him, "I demand in the name of the living God -- tell us if you are the Messiah, the Son of God."

Jesus replied, "You have said it. And in the future you will see the Son of Man seated in the place of power at God's right hand and coming on the clouds of heaven."

"Blasphemy!" Caiaphas shouted, tearing his clothes in anger. "Why do we need other witnesses? You have all heard his blasphemy. What is your verdict?"

"Guilty!" they shouted.

Not having the authority to sentence Jesus to death, Caiaphas sent him to stand trial before the Roman governor, Pilate.

Coming out to meet them Pilate asked, "What is your charge against this man?"
They replied, "This man has been leading

our people astray by claiming he is the Messiah, a king."

Then Pilate called for Jesus to be brought to him. After questioning Jesus, Pilate went out again to the people and told them, "He is not guilty of any crime."

But the Jewish leaders argued saying, "But he is causing riots by his teaching wherever he goes -- all over Judea, from Galilee to Jerusalem!"

Then Pilate announced, "You brought this man to me, accusing him of leading a revolt. Nothing this man has done calls for the death penalty. So I will have him flogged, and then I will release him."

Pilate's soldiers took Jesus away, stripped him of his clothes, and wrapped him in a scarlet robe. Placing a crown of thorns on his head they mocked him saying, "Hail, king of the Jews!"

Then they flogged him as Pilate had commanded.

After they had finished beating Jesus, Pilate returned to the crowd saying, "I am going to bring him out to you now, but understand clearly that I find him not guilty."

The crowd shouted louder and louder, demanding that Jesus be put to death. "Crucify him!" they screamed.

Afraid that a riot might break out, Pilate sent for a bowl of water and washed his hands before the crowd saying, "I am innocent of this man's blood. The responsibility is yours!"

Then Pilate turned Jesus over to to be crucified.

Carrying his own cross the soldiers led Jesus to the place of the Skull. There Jesus was crucified between two criminal.

Pilate had the soldiers nail a sign above Jesus that read, "JESUS OF NAZARETH, THE KING OF THE JEWS."

As Jesus hung on the cross the crowd mocked him saying, "If you are the King of the Jews, save yourself!

Likewise, the religious leaders scoffed, "He saved others, but he can't save himself! Let him come down from the cross right now, and we will believe in him!"

Having compassion on his accusers Jesus responded, "Father, forgive them, for they don't know what they are doing."

As darkness fell across the land, Jesus called out in a loud voice, "My God, my God, why have you abandoned me?"

Knowing that his mission was now

complete Jesus cried out, "Father, I entrust my spirit into your hands!" Then he bowed his head and released his spirit.

At that moment the curtain in the Temple was torn in two, from top to bottom. The earth was shaken and rocks split apart.

Then the Roman officer who stood facing Jesus exclaimed, "This man truly was the Son of God!"

When the crowd who had gathered to see the crucifixion saw what had happened, they went away with broken hearts.

Taking Jesus' body down from the cross his friends wrapped him in sheets of cloth, and laid him in a nearby tomb.

Then a heavy stone was rolled in front of the tomb.

Concerned that Jesus' disciples might come and steal the body Pilate ordered guards to seal the tomb and keep watch day and night.

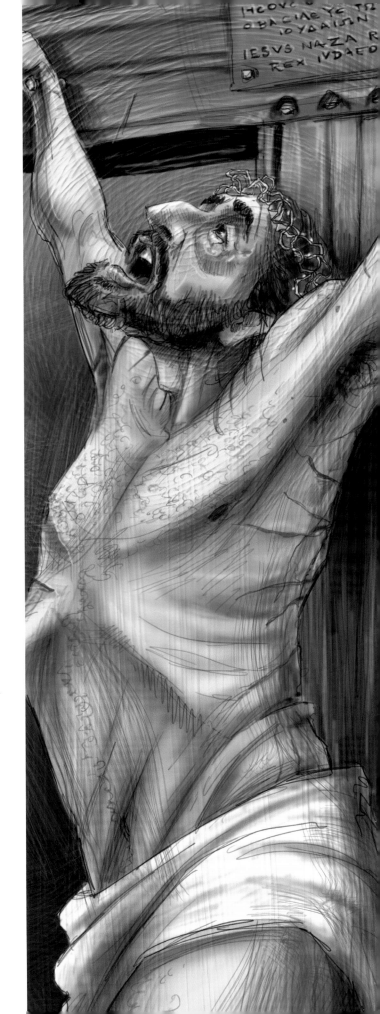

Chapter 13

THE RESURRECTION

Early on Sunday morning, as the new day was dawning, Mary Magdalene went out to visit the tomb.

Suddenly, as she arrived, there was a great earthquake! An angel of the Lord came down from heaven, rolled aside the stone and sat on it. His face shone like lightning, and his cloths were as white as snow.

The guards shook with fear when they saw him, and they fell into a dead faint.

Mary was terrified and bowed with her face to the ground. Then the angel asked, "Why are you looking among the dead for someone who is alive? He isn't here! He is risen from the dead!"

Then Mary entered the tomb and discovered that Jesus' body was no longer there, just as the angel had spoken.

As Mary turned to leave she saw someone standing in the garden. It was Jesus, but she didn't recognize him.

"Dear woman, why are you crying?" Jesus asked her. "Who are you looking for?"

Thinking Jesus was the gardener she replied, "Sir, if you have taken him away, tell me where you have put him, and I will go and get him."

"Mary!" Jesus said.

In that moment Mary recognized Jesus. Overcome with emotion Mary ran to Jesus and embraced him.

As Mary clung to Jesus, he said to her, "Go find my brothers and tell them that I am ascending to my Father and your Father, to my God and your God."

At once Mary left that place and found the disciples telling them, "I have seen the Lord!"

At this, Peter and John ran to the garden tomb.

Entering the tomb they saw the linen wrappings lying where Jesus' body had been laid. At that moment they understood that Jesus had been raised from the dead.

That same day two of Jesus' followers were walking to the village of Emmaus. As they walked along they were talking about everything that had happened.

Suddenly, Jesus appeared and began walking with them, but God kept them from recognizing him.

Jesus asked them, "What are you discussing so intently as you walk along?"

Gripped with sadness they replied, "You must be the only person in Jerusalem who hasn't heard about all the things that have happened there the last few days."

"What things?" Jesus asked.

"The things that happened to Jesus, the man from Nazareth," they said. "He was a prophet who did powerful miracles, and he was a mighty teacher in the eyes of God and all the people. But our leading priests and other religious leaders handed him over to be condemned to death, and they crucified him. We had hoped he was the Messiah who had come to rescue Israel. Then some women from our group of his followers were at his tomb early this morning, and they came back with an amazing report. They said his body was missing, and they had seen angels who told them Jesus is alive! Some of our men ran out to see, and sure enough, his body was gone, just as the women had said."

Then Jesus explained to them from all of Scriptures the things concerning himself.

As they arrived in Emmaus they begged him, "Stay the night with us, since it is getting late."

That evening as they sat down to eat, Jesus took the bread and blessed it. Then he broke it and gave it to them. Suddenly, their eyes were opened, and they recognized him.

And at that moment he disappeared!

Excited to tell the others of their encounter with Jesus they journeyed back to Jerusalem and found the disciples meeting behind locked doors because they were afraid of the Jewish leaders.

As they began to tell their story Jesus himself was suddenly standing there among them.

"Peace be with you," Jesus said.

But the whole group was startled and frightened, thinking they were seeing a ghost!

"Why are you frightened?" he asked. "Why are your hearts filled with doubt? Look at my hands. Look at my feet. You can see that it's really me. Touch me and make sure that I am not a ghost, because ghosts don't have bodies, as you see that I do."

As he spoke, he showed them his hands and his feet. Still they stood there in disbelief, filled with joy and wonder.

One of the twelve disciples, Thomas, was not with the others when Jesus appeared to them.

When they told Thomas, "We have seen the Lord!"

He replied, "I won't believe it unless I see the nail wounds in his hands, put my fingers into them, and place my hand into the wound in his side."

Eight days later while the disciples were together Jesus appeared to them again. This time Thomas as among them.

Jesus said to Thomas, "Put your finger here, and look at my hands. Put your hand into the wound in my side. Don't be faithless any longer. Believe!"

"My Lord and my God!" Thomas exclaimed.

Then Jesus told him, "You believe because you have seen me. Blessed are those who believe without seeing me."

Jesus appeared to his disciples many times over the next 40 days, teaching them about the Kingdom of God.

Thomas

Chapter 14

THE GREAT COMMISSION

As the time drew near for Jesus to return to the Father, Jesus appeared to the disciples along the shore of the Sea of Galilee.

The disciples had been fishing all night and had not caught a single fish.

Jesus called out to them from the shore asking, "Fellows, have you caught any fish?"

"No," they replied.

Then Jesus said, "Throw out your net on the right-hand side of the boat, and you'll get some!"

Following Jesus' instruction the disciples cast their nest on the other side of the boat. As they pulled in the nets they caught such a great number of fish that they could not lift them into the boat.

Realizing it was Jesus who had told them to cast their nets on the other side of the boat, John said to Simon Peter, "It's the Lord!"

When Simon Peter heard that it was Jesus, he jumped into the water, and swam to shore. The others stayed with the boat, pulling the loaded net to the shore.

As the disciples arrived at the shore, they found breakfast waiting for them -- fish cooking over a charcoal fire, and some bread.

"Now come and have some breakfast!" Jesus said. And he served them the bread and the fish.

At this, Jesus gathered his disciples together and said to them, "I have been given all authority in heaven and on earth. Therefore, go and make disciples of all the nations, baptizing them in the name of the Father and the Son and the Holy Spirit. Teach these new disciples to obey all the commands I have given you. And be sure of this: I am with you always, even to the end of the age."

Jesus continued, "Do not leave Jerusalem until the Father sends you the gift he promised, as I told you before. John baptized with water, but in just a few days you will be baptized with the Holy Spirit. And you will be my witnesses, telling people about me everywhere -- in Jerusalem, through-out Judea, in Samaria, and to the ends of the earth."

John 20:20 - 21:25; 1st Corinthians 6:50; Matthew 28:16-20; Mark 16:15-20; Luke 24:44-53; Acts 1:1-12

Then Jesus led them to Bethany. There he lifted his hands towards heaven and blessed his disciples.

As he was blessing them, Jesus was taken up into heaven.

As the disciples strained to see him rising into heaven, two men clothed in white robes suddenly stood among them.

"Men of Galilee," they said, "why are you standing here staring into heaven? Jesus has been taken from you into heaven, but someday he will return from heaven in the same way you saw him go!"

From that day forward the disciples preached the Good News about Jesus everywhere they went. And the Lord worked through them in miraculous ways so that many believed in Jesus and were saved.

The disciples saw Jesus do many other miraculous signs in addition to the ones recorded in this book. But these are written so that you may continue to believe that Jesus is the Messiah, the Son of God, and that by believing in him you will have life by the power of his name.

And now Jesus says to you,

"Come, follow me,
and I will show you
how to fish for people!"

- Spoken by Jesus

"For he has rescued us from the kingdom of darkness and transferred us into the Kingdom of his dear Son, who purchased our freedom and forgave our sins.

Christ is the visible image of the invisible God. He existed before anything was created and is supreme over all creation, for through him God created everything in the heavenly realms and on earth.

He made the things we can see and the things we can't see--such as thrones, kingdoms, rulers, and authorities in the unseen world. Everything was created through him and for him. He existed before anything else, and he holds all creation together.

Christ is also the head of the church, which is his body.

He is the beginning, supreme over all who rise from the dead. So he is first in everything.

For God in all his fullness was pleased to live in Christ, and through him God reconciled everything to himself. He made peace with everything in heaven and on earth by means of Christ's blood on the cross.

This includes you who were once far away from God. You were his enemies, separated from him by your evil thoughts and actions. Yet now he has reconciled you to himself through the death of Christ in his physical body. As a result, he has brought you into his own presence, and you are holy and blameless as you stand before him without a single fault."

-- Written to the followers of Jesus
in Colossae by the Apostle Paul
Colossians 1:13-22 NLT

Paul

MARK LUDY
The Illustrator

Driven by a lifelong obsession with doodling, Mark
is passionate about creating art that captivates the
imagination. As an author and illustrator of 12 picture
books, Mark considers it a privilege to live out his love
for people through his God given gifts. He is a regular
speaker, using humor and insight to encourage and
challenge people of all ages.

Learn more about him, his art and his books
@ MarkLudy.com